Petals of Magnolia

TAMARAH ROCKWOOD

Bainbridge Island Press

Petals of

Magnolia

SECOND EDITION

TAMARAH ROCKWOOD

Bainbridge Island Press

Bainbridge Island, WA

Petals of Magnolia (2nd Edition)
by Tamarah Rockwood
1st Ed Copyright © 2009
2nd Ed. Copyright © 2025
All rights reserved

Published in 2025 by Bainbridge Island Press
Bainbridge Island, WA
https://bainbridgeisland.press

Printed in the United States of America

ISBN: 978-1-961451-13-1
Library of Congress Control Number: 2025950193

Cover & Book Design: Ben Rockwood

9 8 7 6 5 4 3 2 1

Dedicated to my loving husband

CONTENTS

1

2

3

FOREWORD TO THE SECOND EDITION

I have always written poetry, the same as every other poet. We write because we must. We write because there exists within us an insatiable need to speak the unspeakable, to give form to what resists containment by ordinary language. In a way, this book was my debut into speaking.

When I first published *Petals of Magnolia* in 2008, I was a new mother learning to find grace behind leaking coffeepots and uncut lawns. I was a wife crafting a home with careful stitches, terrified they might come undone. I was a poet who didn't yet know she would spend decades devoted to understanding why poetry speaks to us and for us; and how it accomplishes this seemingly impossible task.

My debut collection of poetry was an homage to Walt Whitman's *Leaves of Grass*. Whitman understood that poetry is not decoration but necessity. Not embellishment but truth-telling in its most elemental form. He wrote himself into existence with unflinching attention to the self as a universe worth exploring, teaching subsequent generations of poets that we need not apologize for claiming our small territory in the vast landscape of literature.

I named my book *Petals of Magnolia* to remember the magnolia trees that surrounded my home when I was a girl. Those powerful trees were constant and beautiful through every sunny day and through every storm. I remember staining my fingernails picking out the seeds, the way the petals felt smooth and ivory in my hands, how the tree stood solid while everything around it changed. Poetry should be the same as these trees: the words are petals that guide us through sun and storms alike to mark the path of our human experience.

Poetry occupies a crucial position in the history of human thought. It was founded at the beginning of time and has since evolved through many phases, enduring centuries of philosophical scrutiny. When I think of what poetry should look like, I cannot help but reflect on how many philosophers and critics have attempted to define or dismiss it.

The tension between poetry and philosophy is ancient and productive. Plato explained why he believed poetry was dangerous. Even rubbish. It wasn't truth, he argued in *The Republic*. Poetry corrupted the youth through metaphorical language. A heart is not a red red rose. A grieving mother is not a stone. To Plato, these substitutions were lies, removing us from ultimate reality. Poetry was mimesis twice removed. A copy of a copy.

But Aristotle later took up poetry's banner and defiantly declared in his *Poetics* that "the greatest thing by far is to have a command of metaphor. This alone cannot be imparted by another; it is the mark of genius." And more importantly: "The poet should prefer probable impossibilities to improbable possibilities." Aristotle understood what his teacher could not: that poetry's power lies precisely in its refusal to be literal, in its insistence on the probable impossible over the merely factual.

This philosophical debate speaks to the core of what we do when we write and read poetry. We share our truths through the ancient language of poetry; a language used by prophets, mystics, and poets who translate visions and emotions so that we can understand the nuanced complexities of life. How can we fully understand love without the bloom of the rose? How can we comprehend the weight of grief without the stone? This metaphorical language is not a deviation from truth but a deeper truth itself.

Seventeen years have passed since that first publication. I completed my degree in Creative Writing and Literature at Harvard, became an Academic Researcher at the University of Birmingham pursuing a PhD on the history of the exclamation mark in modernist poetry, and co-founded Bainbridge Island Press, an independent poetry publishing house creating sanctuary for new voices, with my incredible husband, Ben. I am chair for Ars Poetica in western Washington, served as President of ANHW and Chairwoman of the Literary Committee at the Rainier Club, launched the POETICS podcast, and published my second collection, *A, B.* I have five children now, where once I had one toddler collecting kelp bulbs like "priceless blessings/treasures."

A lot has changed in these seventeen years. The beauty has remained.

I have come a long way since 2008, and I am deeply proud of the words I wrote so bravely back then. The woman who wrote *Petals of Magnolia* was not broken, though she felt like "crumbling clay." She was not lost, though she walked through the wilderness. She had the courage to be vulnerable on the page, to expose her wounds and her wonders with equal honesty. She didn't yet have the vocabulary of literary theory or the confidence of academic credentials, but she had something more important: the instinct that poetry matters, that it preserves what might otherwise be lost to time and silence.

Poetry is important. Not only to us now, but to those we have written about who are no longer with us. For future generations searching for meaning in the human experience. By preserving our legacy of language, we participate in the great continuum of human expression. This is what hope looks like: the act of writing down our lives, trusting that our words will matter to someone, somewhere, sometime.

Poetry is truth. Poetry is love. Poetry is essential to our lives.

We are republishing this collection because the poems we write in our youth don't become less true with time. They become more necessary. They remind us where we started, what we survived, how we learned to keep breathing. If you had told that 2008 version of myself that she would become a PhD researcher, publisher, and mother of five who still makes time to write, I don't know if she would have believed you.

But if you had told her that poetry would save her life, that words would be her wilderness and her sanctuary, she would have understood. She already knew.

Welcome back to the garden. The magnolia petals are still here, smooth and ivory and patient. And somewhere, in the morning mist of Edinburgh or the marine fog of the Pacific Northwest, I am still that woman. And I am also someone new. Still believing, with Aristotle, that probable impossibilities are more true than improbable possibilities.

Thank you for being here to celebrate poetry together.

—Tamarah Rockwood

Petals of Magnolia

TAMARAH ROCKWOOD

1

When I consider your heavens,
the work of your fingers,
the moon and the stars,
which you have set in place,
what is man that you are mindful of him.
—King David, *Psalms* 8, v.3-4

PETALS OF MAGNOLIA

I remember

the thick, ivory petals

of magnolia; as a child, I

would stroke the smooth leaf and

in a child's reverie, relax in her simple

beauty. I have grown, and have only

memories of magnolia trees to

remind me of the reverie

which spoke so quietly

and through

me.

SEA WEED

I watched it rip itself from the bottom and float to the surface one marine-foggy day. The amber bulbs floated as buoys for the stalk and leaves that followed the ascent. It was a longish piece from the fringe of the bed of kelp, and it seemed to writhe and struggle against the waves until it could snap its base and untangle itself from the roots which had affixed it to the clump of mud that had been loitering next to an old watch and a bottle of something empty; but the label had come off, and I do not know what substance had lingered within until it had inebriated its possessor enough to let it escape beneath the waves, as well.

I let some breath release from my lungs and I followed the piece of kelp, a little sorry for having to breathe at all, and leaving the reticent peace. My yellow and green fins stirred up some sand on the way up, raising some detached seagrass so a few got tangled on my legs and came along for a free ride. When I got to the surface my mask was a little foggy anyway, so I was able to take it off and spit in it again to keep the mist from collecting. There was a little more foam floating around me than when I first went down, and I figured it was due to the winds picking up and churning the waters a little bit more. I looked back to the shore looking for beach flags to see if I was right: which I was. The lifeguards' pole had a hysterical fabric orange cone attached to the top, as if struggling to break free and warn us all of what it sees looming on the horizon, that only it can see from that vantage point.

The kelp I had followed was floating next to me, some of it draping down the wave it trembled on. It had trapped some of the mocha foam in circlets of stem it had looped in the water, creating little hills of salty fluff. I didn't feel like I was moving, except for the motion of the ocean breathing, raising and lowering me in a gentle lull; yet, when I looked back to see if the orange cone had finally gotten its wish, I saw the towel I had laid down on a mound of sand was much smaller than a few minutes previous. I kissed an amber bulb and wished the kelp the best of fates as it drifted away from us, and decided my own fate would not fare as well if I drifted towards the horizon, so I paddled my fins and headed back to the shore. There was still a few long, dark green strands of seagrass wrapped around me for good luck. I let them come along: who was I to interrupt the destiny of seagrass?

The wind had indeed picked up and it roared in my cold ears. In my trek back, I could only relish with the memory of watching that piece of kelp furiously snap itself and drift away, by itself. It didn't mind the hills of foam that it collected, nor the slight wilting some of its leaves succumbed to by surfacing.

 I swam on my back and watched it
float in the direction of the sun.

GRACE

My quest for grace has been a mighty one
I have been looking all day
Behind the leaking coffeepot,
behind the wall socket that lost a screw and won't stay in the
case flat
just past the mountain of bills;
I searched for grace beyond the uncut lawn
And past the broken mower,
to just behind the clutter in the garage.
Grace seemed to elude me today,
but I kept looking.
I needed it to get me past
The memories of yesterday's fight,
last year's debacle with employment,
I even needed it to get me beyond
The nights I spent cowering in corners
When I was younger,
wondering where God was...
what gentle pasture was he tending, while I
hid in the shadows from drunken demons.
I searched with all my might for this thing called grace,
because without it, all the bills
and all the lost screws
and all the memories seem to topple
and crash on my rag doll fabric
that I had pieced together so carefully.

And the sound of my daughter clumsily
Stomping down the hallway
Stopped my busy mind,
and the gentle touch of my husband's hand on my shoulder
as he was passing by to the garage
broke the wax shell that had been so quickly accumulating
around my tattered rag doll heart
and I could only think of Angels.
Messengers from God, who remind me
That maybe this isn't Eden, and maybe I can't see God in the
garden everyday
Like Adam had the luxury of doing.
But He gave me Angels so I could find the manna of grace
Everyday.

BROKEN SAND

I was sitting on the fine sand and just watching the ocean.
I hadn't been here in a while, and it was nice to return.
I live far away now, and although it stays close to my mind,
it is a long drive.
I watched the ocean foam rustle in the marine breeze, blowing
little tufts onto the clumps of kelp; there was quite a bit of
both that day, making the ocean a little mucky.
I watched a man and his girlfriend enjoying the end of the
day together; him taking pictures of her dancing in the
waves, unyielding, uninhibited; her deep skin reflecting
her dark bronze bikini, which matched the murky waves
unceremoniously. She raised her hands and smiled and
twirled, as if she was 12 again. They both looked so happy;
that is what the ocean can do to your soul, I've found.
I watched a tanned woman read a thick book while sitting
at the foot of a lifeguard station. She was wearing a purple
strapless dress that didn't cover much else besides her bathing
suit; but that was okay at the beach. She wrestled with the
wind, who insisted she read the next two chapters quickly;
but she calmly laid them back down and continued with her
one page. She was lovely to watch, a stillness around her
which kept her eyes steady while her hair was not.
I watched my own daughter struggle with her steps in the
sand. She was still younger than two, and running wasn't
as easy as she found it was on a lawn. She collected kelp
bulbs and gave them to me, her dad, her uncle, as priceless
blessings/treasures.

I kept my hands in the fine sand; I could not stop running the grains past my fingers; they felt like silk compared to the rough dirt clods I have in my garden at home. I started breaking the sand on the top, where a high wave had come earlier and dried in the sun. I broke the layer and softly ground it into the sand. I used to do this when I was younger, when I lived closer. But now when I tapped the thin tier, I thought back to the years I spent on this sand before; while watching my daughter twirl the long strands of kelp in the wind, as if they were her own silk streamers, as they had been mine.

I sat on the fine sand and just watched the ocean.

I hadn't been here in a while, and it was nice to return.

I live far away now, and although it stays close to my mind, it is a long drive.

CRUMBLING CLAY

When my past cannot be contained
after all the suppression is breached,
it slowly leaks beyond my sternum and
eeks beyond the pale of my skin;
through the pores, covering my flesh
contaminating the aura of cleanliness I had
so fretfully maintained.
I am a rotten woman,
rotting from the inside,
pickled with despair and fortitude,
a mass of crumbling clay
in the shape of a
good Christian woman.

AMBER DUST

I always imagined him coming down a dusty dirt road at the beginning of summer, gales of amber dust swirling behind him.

PENUMBRA DEOSCULATION

Raining;
Hailing.
My fellow worshippers and I.

At the eve of morn,
Our necks crane back,
our noses to the sky;

The beckon of Glory's vision:
The breaking of our quotidian.

Our silence prevails, and our lorn
Bids haste: Eve's shadow diminishes quick.
Our time is short with these celestial swishes.

Raining;
Hailing;
God's confetti kisses.

BUTTERFLIES AND DRAGONS

A window image
Of your pale face stays
Stained in me. I imagine
immature scenarios in which I
rescue you, and bestow
my kiss to you.
It was the moment.
That is my excuse.

I frame you
As a picture for
The mantle in my mind: above
The hidden dragon fires. The stained
Colors crackle, speaking back
To me. Telling me
You remember the first time,
too,
that you spoke my name.
Butterflies on your lips
Fluttered into my hands
And enabled them to write
Your name.
What's in a name.
I cannot pronounce yours,
and my mute communication
is all I have to give you.

CRICKET

Even I hardly understand
The devotion of my work.
I have no crown, no tiara;
I have not been issued a halo.
The toils of my labor
Viciously rip
My soul's threads,
so the beads bounce off
the waxed linoleum floor.

I have patience until I'm ill.
I have tolerance while I sweat.

My ethical cricket is silenced.
My blind eye is johnny-on-the-spot.

One more emotion-of-the-week.
One more hurdle to leap.
One more sudden relative to tolerate.

STEEL WALLS

Like the lump in my throat
That I can't avoid,
or the headache accumulated over
time; I can pacify myself
and my lump for a while.
I can tread in denial,
I can put it aside.
But on overcast days, when
I can't run outside...
I'm stuck within the room
I've carved for myself, with
Steel walls and painful floors.
Perhaps it was easy for you
To leave your room, your past,
yourself;
the process has not been so simple
for me.
You have moved on, and one
Out of three is good enough to pacify you.
While I still pacify this
One lump in my heart.

SECRET SUTURES

This is not a rosy picture
painted for me. Fragrant petals
are not strewn in my room,
and my peaceful molasses growth
is enough. For now
it is enough
         My secret sutures I harvest
on my own.
         And, to be honest with you, with
myself, your healing is magic
to me; a sleight of hand
manipulation of altar smoke.
The inhalation of these healing mists
is not something I can understand.
The woman, happy after her
mother's death;
The woman, happy after her
abusive marriage.
The woman, happy after her
tormented childhood.
The woman, happy after her
soul had been destroyed.
Tell me what herb to smoke, what
liquid to drink, what solvent
to apply. Because my soul
cries no.

My soul cries no.
The altar call for healing,
for hope, for a future of sun;
I stay.
The prescription for redemption;
I am rooted in the desert
with the Israelites,
rebellious and defiant with pain.

My tapered growth will last.
My soul cries no.
Because I loved once, and I hoped
twice, and fire consumed me.
The fires tested my spirit, and
the gold did not remain, but
the straw burst into green flames.
My passion for sealed sutures is
cold, frozen in the iceberg of
my sea.
But it is intact, preserved, even when
my soul cries no.

I refuse.
Because I am defined by my pain.
I endured for God, and to
these moments of terror,
I cling.
I refuse hope,
because I am lost in the desert
of dry, quiet sobs. But this has been my
dwelling for years. This is
my comfort zone.
Because it is mine.
And I refuse.

It is as if by every minute
that I wait for it to end,
another layer is stripped off,
and I am yet raw again.
The wails of others, re experiencing
their torment before the pews
strips faster, and my own
anguish is echoing in my ears,
until a feedback loop

forces me outside
to regroup,
and scale back.

And then what.
Perchance I do revisit my horror.
And then what.
What magic trick will remove
the pin cushion heart of mine.
What astounding feat
will break the firm mold of
skepticism, of cynicism, I have
spent so much time welding.
And then what.
What plated dragon can test
my armor'd defenses?
What equation of hope can You offer.
Perchance I do give in.
Perchance I do soften.
Perchance I do feel healed.
And then,
What.

Selah

My exercise of faith.
An hour of praying,
of pleading,
for mercy. For holy mercy on my
resistant soul, who for too long
has sat as a fixed steel statue.
　　　I go deeper into the stretch.
But, eventually, the heat from His embrace
has penetrated my cool skin, and
I am enveloped by his white taffy cradle,
tenderly secure in the peace of
His manifested love.
　　　I lean farther away from me.

Selah

HIS SANCTUARY

The rocks below do not intimidate
me, nor does the white water, fresh
off the melted snow, chill my blood.
Wild animals may linger here, yet I
pace my steps toward Heaven.
My compass may fall from my hand,
my ship may no longer see land,
my ears may never hear
the angels in the estuary, yet
I will travel bravely through to
His Sanctuary.

ESCAPE VELOCITY UNDER MY NEEDLE

I feel secure now.

After years of work, sewing
Bits and pieces together, ripping
Away old cloth, double-stitching some seams
To ensure their longevity:

I feel secure now.

After molding the material to place
Inside this rag-doll image I created;
Forming different shapes over time, and
Knowing this, too, will continue to change:

I feel secure now.

After affixing my rag-doll creation
To another rag-man, equally as
Malleable, changeable, and fully lovable –
Becoming a set, a pair, and unremovable:

I feel secure now.

After we created a little doll of our own,
and built this doll-house in which to live.
After fulfilling my desires to seek out
Knowledge, love, compassion, and God;

And after accepting that some cloths
Of mine will have to be restitched again,

that this changing rag-doll has help
to restitch and restuff. After all this:

I feel secure now.

2

He makes me lie down in green pastures,
he leads me beside quiet waters,
he restores my soul.
—King David, *Psalms* 23, v.3

All religions, arts and sciences are branches
of the same tree. All these aspirations are
directed toward ennobling man's life, lifting
it from the sphere of mere physical existence
and leading the individual towards freedom.
—Albert Einstein

WINDS OF ME

The edge is so near
I can feel the rush of wind
gusting in wild gales, nearly sucking me in;
The edge was where I had come,
and the edge was so near.
What does it all mean?

If I was a child, I would be playing under the swings
after the rain;
If I was rich, I would be celebrating my life
aboard a yacht, the Santa Maria, discovering
wild islands and foreign tongues.
If I had all the stars in the sky, maybe I would
halo myself with daisy chains of universes and time.

But I have the Gregorian calendar
tattooed on my wrinkled face,
as crushed, stained rose-colored paper
fitted over a terrible mortal skull, reminding
me of the time I have spent,
of the time I have.

Behind me lay the barren soil of my life.
I had worked so hard, and yet
despite every bead of sweat I endured,
every person I knew, every good deed, every mistake,
every unanswered question,
I have still brought myself here.

As I look up
and the breeze overtakes my breath,
and I can feel my heart slow to the beat of
the storm clouds marching across the sky.
I heard every story my grandmother told me

of "forever" and "eternity" and "everlasting love,"
but I wonder if there is any proof of forever,
I thought I would have seen it in my life.

What is beyond this divide.
Will a gleaming city house me?
Will the crux of life end beyond this cliff?
What will become of me,
as I hardly know what I am looking for,
or who I am when I am alone.
But still the angel said to the women:
Do not be afraid, for
I know you are looking for Jesus.

I close my eyes and
in my mind I watch the rugged cross
being drug through the dirt, laced with his blood.
I shudder, for even I have not suffered so much;
and yet, I suffer so much.
In my mind I can feel the nails crash violently into my skin,
feel the shallow breaths slowly leave me,
I feel the cries from the women who cower beneath the
shadow
of the cross.
And yet, the angel said to them:
Do not be afraid.
I know you are looking for Jesus;
at the edge of my life,
when the winds of change sweep me off my stubborn feet,
at the edge of my mind when the upheaval of thoughts
crumble on my
flimsy excuses,
and when the meaning of my strife
drifts like smoke on the still river of life;

I feel the answers my grandmother spoke,
softly floating in my haze
and drifting along the river that
winds through life's valley.
When I stop worrying about my own mortal swim
and what he means to me
I see how much greater is the purpose
of how much I mean to Him.

IN THE WILDERNESS

In the wilderness
begins my walk across the baked earthen floor.
The sun's gaze was so much greater
with no tree or building to hide me;
the ground has not had rain
and is as parched as my soul;
Even the hungry wind barely carries
the meager dust and pollen from
desert flowers, somewhere in the distance.
      Somewhere in the distance
I can see some desert flora
hiding in the heat waving on the ground.
It seems, the dry yet fertile land around me
holds many seeds, but they lay in a
dormant sleep under my feet
until they find the grace in the clouds.
There is no harvest. I can barely scrape
a handful of dirt in my hands.
There are cloudless skies.
There is no rain.
There are no shadows under which to hide.
      There are no shadows under the sun,
no where to escape, no hiding place I can see.
In the middle of the desert,
I have found myself.
My heart is searching for something
incredible; and yet, I have walked into
the barren land which can't even grow shadow.
My mind feels lost, being so exposed.
Yet this rouge shape that sits on the horizon
compels me to continue.

I am compelled to continue,
because if I sit, I will be lost in the wilderness
for the eternity of my soul. But this blush of hope on the horizon
beckons me with such burning intrigue
I can only heed its call.

When I reach the plant, nay a foot high in person
I tower over its beauty,
which called to me from across the entire desert.
This prickled desert rose, such an unusual presence in a
place of barren thoughts;
Her purpose was not to be beautiful unto herself,
but to use the barren land around her
to show the enormous beauty
God could fit into something so small.

God could fit into something so small as my heart
a longing for Him so great
that I will travel across entire lands to find Him.
And it was not the footsteps which brought
my spirit to the steep;
it was The Spirit as my rose:
it was The Spirit in my feet.

At times when a wilderness consumes
my heart, and the only hiding place
to be found is within
an idea or space,
sometimes it was placed for us,
by the guiding hands of Jesus.

THRESHOLD OF HEAVEN

Maestro:
I offer you my green palms
to be laid down at your noble feet.
I give you my life
to be triumphantly filled with
your love;
Lord, your way is worthy,
and I celebrate your holy name,
which is embroidered so boldly
within my illuminated soul.
Your brilliant light from Heaven
shines mercifully upon our
wandering path
as a pillar of illuminated hope.
Your angel's ethereal melodies
waft gently down in tender waves
softly strumming the foliage of the forests,
so the whole earth hears
the same praises which
resonate in the timbre of my soul.
Illuminate my heart Maestro,
the way you illuminate the Heavens.

Tell me about heaven.
Tell me about the streets lined with gold.
Tell me about the crystaled rivers of life.
Tell me all your angels names,
and show me where you've hidden them,
here.

I saw the glint of gold on my own path,
and I know what it was.
I saw the splendor of crystal reflections
off the waters surface;
and I saw the remnant of a kiss
from your angel
hovering on the windowsill of my child's room
and I know whose it was.

Maestro:
Splendor is thy dance
when you move in me. Splendor is
the sweet fragrance that
dances on the melodied winds of Heaven.
In the beautiful gypsy winds
I dance
in the illumination of God.
        I can still feel the warmth of Heaven
in the city that almost forgot His love.
and it's good to be in love near
        the threshold of Heaven;
and this is it:
this is it.

ISAIAH SIX

With quiet steps, I tread onto the revered
red carpet, which took me, hushed, to the
illuminated steps, which I could not
bring my heavy feet to tread onto.
My lead knees anchored me to the floor, and
With quiet breaths, I whispered my souls' plea.

Then just beyond the illumination
I saw Father God sitting on a throne,
High and exalted, and the train of His
Robe filled the temple. Above the throne stood
seraphim; each one had six wings: with two
he covered his face, with two he covered
his feet, and with two he flew. And one cried
to another and said: Holy, holy,
holy is the Lord of hosts; The whole earth
is full of His glory!" And the posts of
the door were shaken by the voice of the
one who cried out, and the house was filled with smoke.

And, trembling, I wept, for I knew what
defiance led my heavy feet to this
scarlet-stained altar, for it was my sins
which struck the nails securely. And with my
head hung, I said to myself: "I am undone,
for I know I am a woman of
unclean lips, and I live among people
of unclean lips; And now I have seen the Lord,
My Father, and I feel the beams of my
Soul shake. I am neither worthy nor
Honorable, and the shuddering tears
I pour onto His step are not enough
To wash away the ugly stain which I
Feel branded onto my skin, my heart. The

Stain which sucks the breath from my own lungs and
Replaces cool air with fumes of sulfur."

Then one of the seraphim flew to me,
having in his hand a hot coal which he
had taken with the tongs from the altar;
And he touched my mouth with it, and said:
"Behold, this has touched your lips; Your sinfulness
is taken away, And your sin is cleansed."

I could only lift my head to look at
this angel who had brought a sunset red
ray of hope for my distressed heart. Who had
the authority to bring this ribald
woman anything other than accusing judgment?

But suddenly there was a gust which swept
over my kneeling step and I felt my
lungs expand with breath, and the tears were dried,
without my hands wiping them away in shame.
My branded skin was glowing, and I felt
the pillars of my heart stand bravely; and
I felt the lead of my knees soften to flesh, once more.

And I heard the voice of the Lord, saying:
"Whom shall I send, And who will go for Us?"
Who shall He send? My hands reached out on their own
And in my own face, I could feel a change:
I was smiling, no, I was brimming with
a rainbow of happiness and with my new,
clean mouth, I cried, I shouted to my Father:
"Here am I! Send me."

I HAVE NO MEMORY

I have no memory of being a slave.
The sun has burnt off the memory,
after forty years of walking
my slow, winding course;
I have no memory
of being a slave:
the times I recall belong
to the quiet mornings of the desert,
when animals fled to the shade
of the low bushes
to survive just one more day;
when there wasn't enough wind
to blow the pollen out of the flowers,
and when the children
were too excited to
see Canaan's walls
than to remember their parents stories
of a land beyond the river.
I have no memory of being
a slave.
No sunburnt skin
maps the travels I have seen.

As I see the land beyond
the crumbled walls -
I cannot remember anything
beyond the joshua tree
behind me.

THE MANY NAMES OF JESUS

Who knew the name that would
speak my name in the skies,
Who knew what name would strike the brilliant light of the
sun
and banish the clouds in my eyes.
Who knew
it would be the Almighty,
the Word of God, the Author of Life,
the Good Shepherd and the Morning Star;
Who knew it was the man who was named
the Heir of All Things, The Lamb of God, The Light of the
World
the King Eternal, The King of Ages,
The King of Kings.
Whose name breaks the restraints that kept my heart
from flying above the lofty clouds?
He who speaks to the many sides of me;
He who beholds the many sides of beauty:
The man who gave his life for us:
The many names of Jesus.

HER MEADOW

How tame her flowers seem,
flecked with orchid hues
and smitten with deep amber nectars;
  and yet when the sun is at
  its highest peak in the clear cerulean
  and shines its brightest rays
  into her protected pasture,
  which lays fiercely guarded by
  God's mighty evergreens
  who almost ripple the blue
  with their needled helmets;
in the beautiful rays, her own
melody of wildflowers
rise their roseate petals
and suspend their poetic beauty
for the weary refugees who find
their way to her pined sanctuary;

  her beautiful welcome
  unfolds into a meadow
  of ruby poppies and sapphire lilies;
  little jewels of Heaven, tenderly breathing
  verdant, sylvan sighs upon
  the injured sojourner;

She brings them an epoch
of hushed, divine peace -
So close to Heaven
in her protected prairie
blooming with
God's wildflowers.

GRACES

Into whose ears have my prayers sighed, and why;
what wanton gifts did I receive in grace,
past the beat of my mind as it gave chase
to rest in my humid day. Into whose eye
did the image of my kneeling figure
reflect, and into whose arms was I held?
The fury of the storm in my beast, quelled
still by the grace of my God, my healer.
Thus in the desert stands the broken tree,
healed by clean rain, binding splintered flesh;
pure water from Heaven, poured lavishly
into its torrid trunk, yields bronze from mesh.
Unmerited love, poured upon my face;
tenacious charity, rooted in grace.

MY POT

The angel said to the women:
Do not be afraid, for
I know you are looking for Jesus.
Like shovels of soil thrown into my pot,
my troubles have overwhelmed me,
and I cannot see.
My courage leaves me, and I hold
still in the soil.
I am depleted and tender,
but though I face fear in my
sodden solitude,
I put my bulb of trust in the Lord.
I am hurt, and He thinks of me.
I reach my eager, green fingers
through the dirt, and I search;
I hear,
the noise of the world, and the
noisome tales on the air.
I see
secular stories of my world,
of His world.
I seek
books searching for meaning
where I do find volumes of drivel.
Through all the mud and muck

I climb through
sifting and sorting, on
my search for truth:
on the air, in the world, through absurdity -
and when my green leaves
burst through the potted soil,
and grab the Lord's warm rays -
I raise my white lily head
and proudly reclaim the pot as
my own, sifted in righteousness.
I heard him say when I was below:
Do not be afraid,
I know you are looking for Jesus.
I was looking,
and my rapturous spirit has arisen with Him
on this Easter day.

I CRY FOR MORE

What vision of the astral doorway is given
that I see the fiery clouds lining
the heightened ceiling of Heaven?

Whose brilliant eye is upon my upturned face
Mine alone, soaking in the peopled sea
of His busy golden terrace.

What celestial ears can only hear
My feeble voice, nearly lost on this
dusty earthen sphere.

And whose love is it that I explore?
Into His Fatherly embrace,
I cry for more.

More, bring to me.
More love to my family.
More grace from Your gentle hand,
More fruit from our barren land.
More comfort for the weak and weary,
More praises from the joyed and teary
More salvation for Your children, come.
More to Your reprieve, shall we succumb.
More worship from my lips adore:
More love for You,
I cry for more.

I CAN FEEL

I can feel:
I can feel Your outstanding love
throughout my out-stretched hands;
Your brilliant love that I see
hidden in sunbeams, creeping slowly over me
until I am wholly engulfed by Your comforting Spirit.
I can feel:
I can feel relief soften
my rough edges, during moments
when I think I can feel
every shard of broken clay
scrape my raw skin, worn thin from
wearily toiling for so long now.
Your Godly love calms the storm I feel
in my soul, and stills the ache,
the knot, the pain. And once again:
I can feel. I can feel my own love, rising above
my heart, beyond the lump in my throat, and
emerges as a mighty cry of victory,
praising Your name, Your power, Your love.
I can feel the brilliance of Your Spirit
shine through my once feeble body,
which is now healed and beautiful.
When once I was hurt, once I was torn, once I was numb;
Yet beneath the sutures, your radiant love has shone and
healed every wound;
Shone from You, who knew everything I have ever done;
And when the fury of the storm was quieted
by the faith of my outstretched hands:
I can love,
and I can feel.

MY FATHER'S TREE

In my fathers yard there grows a tree:
it was planted not by hands,
it was planted by the wind,
In my fathers yard there grows a tree
which began its life
nearly hidden in the light
dwarfed by the flowers nearby,
sheltered in the shade of the lazy afternoon.
I watched this tree in my fathers yard
feel the warmth of the sun
it could not see,
and grow so faithfully
into this little tree.
In my fathers yard where the garden grows
The gardener watches the young
who need the generous eye;
when the heat is too much,
when the wind is too rough,
when the solitude is too quiet.
I grow in my fathers yard
with firm roots that hold my ground;
although I am touched by those around me,
It is by my gardeners hand
that I flourish and abound.
There is a righteous tree
that stands by me
when the world shifts from soft to hard
but I am fed by the fathers love
in my fathers yard.

MORNING GARDEN

My early black cup,
sipped in front of clear rose dew;
I wake, white with God.

HUNGER

Bow down Your ear, o Lord, hear me; for I am poor and needy.
Be merciful to me, Lord, for I cry to You all day long.
Lord, I lift up my soul.
Give ear to my plea; and attend to the voice of my humble prayer.
In the day of my trouble I will call upon You, for You will answer me.

—Psalms 86

I have been tempted:
By things and people and ideas and wishes...
I am tempted.

I fear Him:
I fear wrath and anger and unforgiveness.
For my paltry heart winces into seclusion.

I pray to my God:
I pray for mercy and wisdom, and strength.
I pray for hope.

I mediate on the marvel when Jesus
was tempted by Satan for so long, and He ate nothing.
He had no fellowship and He had no spiritual food.
And when the days had ended, He was hungry.
I look within myself,
and the shell of a woman I have always seen
overflowing with bitterness and confusion;
I look closer into the darkness, and
With my challenging eyes
I realize it has been empty
For so long.
And the bitterness and fury I thought were pulling
At the seams of my mind, were merely echos
Which I have not been able to quiet on my own.

I hunger.

And so, with ravenous hands, I cling
To the Holy Spirit, and I let
It dwell within me.
And when I search for my echos,
I am greeted with a brilliant light
Which first burned my naked, callow eyes,
and then the warmth emanated from between the
corners and creaks and crevices, and
gently gave my cold hands warmth.

And I am not tempted.
Not by things or people or ideas;
For I am aided by His generous children,
And I am comforted by an Awesome God.

And I do not fear Him.
I do not fear anger or wrath or unforgiveness,
for I am received by a godly fellowship,
and I am forgiven by a forgiving God.

And I pray to my God.
I pray for mercy and strength and hope,
For I have faith in His love,
And I am complete in His church.

When Jesus rebuked Satan and declared
That we should worship the Lord our God,
and serve only Him...
instead of our fears and inhibitions...
The devil left Jesus,
and angels came to help him.

When the Spirit falls down upon me
in an awesome crash
overwhelming my heart until

I am only able to cry in
uncompromising praises of celebration:
Word, you are holy!
You are holy in my life,
You are holy in our church.
I can feel mountains
being raised up, and Your
incredible light blesses the
crests, until the springs have no
recourse other than to pour
your blessings down the
Heavenly slopes, washing away
the loose debris until all..

...that was left in your sight
were gleaming crests of a mighty mountain,
on which is imprinted your Word.
which can be seen
from below, from earth, from Heaven.
Father, Your spirit is welcome
on my heart, to wash away
the debris and leave only
a pure, whole heart which
praises Your holy name,
the name imprinted so boldly
on my illuminated soul.

SWEETER CAKES

I don't know about you
But I am ecstatic, swimming in
tea and centerpieces and heels.
I don't know about you, or
your profession, your faith, your life,
and though your spangled language falls
on my potato ears, I see our children
playing eagerly in the same yard behind us.
I don't know about your
foreign ways, your sweeter cakes, and
mysterious handshakes. I don't know,
or, I am not sure what brought us here;
some magnificent ethereal hand,
guiding our potato paths together;
and together we learn: languages
and cultures and motions and
the Spirit - through the Spirit.
And we, through a crowd of eager noise,
and with mysterious handshakes,
meet in the Spirit,
over our sweeter cakes.

THE ANGEL

I look in your face, and I charge you
with the word I have been given.
I appear before you as words;
words which will give you the destiny
you will embody, because it is yours
to behold. The heavenly scene I have
witnessed, I bring unto you as a
pillar of flame. Just as Moses was the
bearer of words for the people in the desert,
so do I bear words for you, children of God.
There is a messenger who stands above you,
and presides over His house.
There is a messenger who smiles above your smile,
with folded arms and extended wings.
I have seen him.
His message was not for my life, nor for my future;
I am the vessel to carry his charge,
and I bring it to you.
I meditated on the vision of this
behemoth of an angel
who stands at the end of the aisle.
His head reaches the heights of the building;
his wings fill the sanctuary;
his royal blue robes cascade from his shoulders to the floor,
and his scarlet sash lays passionately across his chest
as an ephod for our church.

Just as an angel was sent to the people in the desert
to guide them into a holy place;
the people went so willingly after him,
following the pillar of fire he took with him,
faithful in their steps and willing in their gifts;
Our steps have been seen before us,
and we have been told where we are to go.
And this angel,
the angel Uriel,
is our pillar of fire to lead us
into a holy place
that we are now
prepared to enter.

PRUNING THE ROSE

On my kitchen sill sits my little pots.
Three in a row sprout little violets,
one supports a stem with a few sparse green
leaves. But my crimson jewel sits primly
in the middle: there is my little rose.

It was small and full when I brought it home.
I tried it in a few different spots
Around the house, but it did not flourish.
But next to fellow blossoms, it began
To stretch its green neck towards the sunlight.

Over time it bloomed beautiful blood-red
Buds which grew higher and faster; however,
by then only scattered sections remained
green; And, figuring that it seemed to be
doing so well, despite the mass of dead
leaves and stems, wrought with thorns, I just left it.

It fared through the remainder of winter
Very well, sprouting one petalled precious
At a time. I still left the dead thorns to
Hide the rest of the fresh foliate; it
was part of the rosebush, and I feared pruning.

Spring eventually warmed the sky, and my
Wandering violet sprout began to yield
Tiny pink buds; just one at a time, the
Fragile florets woke and blushed five fingers.
Inspired by this sudden permission
Of anxious regrowth, and with nimble zeal,
I fervently began pruning the rose.

Four maiden roots were planted in her pot,
yet only one crept up the kitchen glass;
yearning, searching, living only to see
the warm Spring sun. How could I not be moved
by her green devotion; through the winter
she silently grew behind the facade
of lifeless branches, and now she reigns higher
than the violets; as though the rose meekly
heard the voice of God through the slated sunlight:
„I am the true vine, and my Father is
the vinedresser. Every branch in Me that
does not bear fruit He takes away, and every
branch that bears fruit He prunes so that it may
bear more fruit...abide in Me and I in
you. As the branch cannot bear fruit itself,
unless it abides in the vine, neither can
you, unless you abide in Me." –Jesus.

She kept her spot next to the low lavender
Perennial, but I placed the clay pot,
in which she had burst to life, within a
worthier basket, to enhance and extol
the radiant life I found behind the thorns.

THE CHRISTIAN MONTAGE:
MY STAINED GLASS WINDOW

As the vernal Christian artist,
we create our stained glass window,
through our loves and our lives; we coexist
in our Father's kaleidoscope meadow.

After a day that has seemed to be a week,
I will still glorify Your name in my heart
And I serve you in my home.

After the kids catch each other's colds
I sanctify my home in Your grace
And I serve you through my children.

After the dog gets out and comes back wet, muddy and late
I will praise the blessings You bring
And I will worship You for Your intervention.

After almost colliding with a speeding car
I eagerly praise Your mightiness
And I worship your alert protection.

In my Christian cathedral,
I let the praise of your righteousness pour through
my brilliant window and declare Your name in my soul's seal,
In my crystal creation I gladly glorify you
exalted and above.
I will proclaim through my mosaic display
the greatness of Your love.
I celebrate you as a spouse, as Your child, in my artistic part;
And although I praise you throughout my spirit and
Throughout my life,
I rage in worship
Within my heart.

CHRIST'S SIRENS

Perched on the carpeted cliff,
seas of blue pews before them,
Promising the moon to wearied sailors.
The sacred harbor of salvation
seems to engulf the Siren's songs
of promise and praise.
      Perched on the porch of Heaven,
singing with voices of trained angels,
guiding worried voyagers to dock,
to Heaven,
to Home.

3

A bird doesn't sing because it has an answer,
it sings because it has a song.
—Maya Angelou

What lies behind us and what lies before
us are tiny matters compared to what lies
within us.
—Ralph Waldo Emerson

Life is to be lived. If you have to support
yourself, you had bloody well better find
some way that is going to be interesting. And
you don't do that by sitting around wonder-
ing about yourself.
—Katherine Hepburn

QUONDAM RAIN

And it's peaceful when it rains;
when the wind and showers drown out the
noisome cars two streets away;
when the birds hide under backyard
rainforest canopies of magnolia,
and as the clouds slowly, calmly drift overhead;
we rest inside, behind thin glass, and slowly
breathe little faces onto the panes; hers just a little
smaller than mine.

And it's peaceful within the rain;
it's too quiet to play anything loud inside,
or worry about going out, since we can't
find the only umbrella.
So we stay behind our thin glass, and I listen
to the river sounds in the treed canopies,
and the monitor which projects her little
songs from down the hall.

And we slowly collide on the couch, shifting
our peaceful weight over each other, to the
rhythm of the river;
and our handmade raft, which once carried Huck,
floats upstream, through the tangle of magnolia
and beyond the sedentary birds to
the quiet quondam of respite;
And we hold hands as our small faces
nod off.

PATH TO THE COAST

The old stomping grounds;
a little weathered, some steps missing,
but the path is still there.
The old journey to the sea;
a little more crooked, a little more beaten,
but the path is still there.
The childish wanderings of my feet,
of the wind, drew us to some sea, I knew not where,
yet the path is still there.
The cheerful days of innocence and frogs,
pickle jars and broken spokes; my red bike is gone,
but the path is still there.
The years I spent dreaming of wandering
down those broken steps with you, even when you
were gone; I would search the winds for your perfume;
My heart being as ragged as the steps to the shore,
yet the path is still there.

VISITATION RIGHTS

Muse #1, please step down.
Administer my poetic crown.
Once a month; this week:
Thrice.
Why not every half hour?
Or Saturday nights?
Instead, I am whored
By your paid visits;
Only when it suits you.
This time: in a tub.
Last week: in class.
I will only whine whilst
You continue this way.
Should you never come,
however,
I will complain to management.

THE ANGEL'S GARDEN

We will hide in the garden, and when the rain ends, we will hide in the bushes, and when the sun shines, we will hide in the trees, and when the night falls, we will hide under the covers and listen for them.

We will hide in the garden until the shouts of their mothers are louder than the sound of the bees landing, precariously, on their tiny fingers.

We will hide in the garden while we watch characters pass through; and when Jean Valjean has stolen the Bishop's candlesticks, we will giggle and wait for him to return.

We will hide in the garden while Eve's confused tears wash the core of her sin, while mothers plant potatoes to feed her children, while Jesus prays through his final hour; Until the tree's boughs cannot bear us any longer. Until the sound of traffic overcomes the trill of the wren:

We will hide
in the garden.

THE HANGMAN'S GALLOWS

If we were children, we would be playing under the swings.
If we were rich, we would be celebrating our anniversary
aboard our yacht, the Santa Maria, discovering
wild islands and foreign tongues.
If we had all the stars in the sky, maybe we would
halo ourselves with daisy chains of universes and time.

But we have the Gregorian calendar
tattooed on our wrinkled faces,
as crushed, stained rose-colored paper
fitted over terrible mortal skulls, reminding
us of the time we could have spent together.

And instead of celestial daisy chains,
you hand me your ring
in front of the Scottish hangman's gallows.

THE WINGED MINSTREL OF LOVE

On a summer evening some time ago
I sat in my garden watching the sun
creep through the fence and illuminate the
Green gold leaves which fluttered as a tender
Symphony, to introduce the evening's star.
The warm zephyr breeze that carried the song
From the boughs to my heart, brought a tiny
Bird to the same branches. He sang as only
A nightingale could sing; a solo
Melody of what he has seen from his heights;
  Of serenades he has witnessed behind
Sun-drenched fences on similar summer eves.
I listened to his sonnets of butterflies
And dragons, swimming in backyard pools of
Perfumed kisses and love notes, clandestinely
Sealed with love. In his song he remembered
Glittering dragons who paraded the
Azure skies, sending their own mighty songs
Of love along the same breeze which carried
The fluttering gold butterfly to dance
On his wings. Such an unparalleled pair,
to the common eye; but the nightingale knew;
He had seen this winged love before. And as
The tiny cupid messenger finished
His epic ballad of poetic romance,
and as I watched the sun creep behind the fence,
my heart was only illuminated
by the faint stars, and the glow radiating
from within the quiet chorus of love
songs which lingered on the breeze long after
 the traveling minstrel had, himself, fluttered
off; following the trail of perfumed kisses.

THE TROLL

The troll who passes under this bridge
      travels safely, hidden under
      the cloak of Nature. His footsteps
      blend in next to marks
      of droves of hooves.
      His foul breath cannot be seen on
      cold mornings: it has no heat.

The troll who passes my door
      carries with him a flock of night,
      as a swarm of biting flies,
      which darkens the sky and
      slowly maws the light.

The troll who eats little girls
      in the Underground, and beats little boys
      with the bones,
      will always return to the belly of the bridge,
      watching weary travelers look over the rail,
      wondering if their Mothers' tales of this beast
      were true.

UNHOPE

He tore his sweet blue eyes out
Until all he saw was red.

LIONS

Lions, giraffes, tigers
Pink, green, yellow – move by her
Rise and fall slumber.

OUR FOREST

How many steps have we yet had, and why
have they taken us through this shaded wood.
How many minutes and miles have we spent
on this leaf covered path, following the
Scottish breath of Spring; How many moments
have we stopped and whispered what even the
tiny birds cannot hear, perched in the lush
canopy of Our Forest. What silences
harbor our likened smiles, our sweetened breath
our clasped hands, our oaths until death. What compass
could have brought us here, which map knows this beat;
which wind blows this way, which Angel guards our feet:

Through the grove our love guides, through calm and unrest,
And we will walk peacefully through Our Forest.

MY LITTLE PAINTED BOX

There is a powder
which turns into the most exquisite tea
when mixed with hot water.
It is in a little metal box, and is
quite expensive. I had never
bought one for myself, until now.
I allowed this painted box to grace
a shelf in my home, and to be taken down
only for special occasions.
I enjoyed one, maybe two cups, since I bought it,
cherishing each expensive drop
as if I were drinking gold.
My husband was curious why my face
was so calm at the end of a busy day,
being clouded by this scented steam;
and I let him hold my
little painted box.

There was an expiration date on the bottom.
I had never noticed it before.

My cups of gold were to expire in 1 week.
At first, I was devastated to learn
of my box's mortality.
But then,
I made myself another cup
(2 in one night!)
and decided to enjoy these cups of gold
enormously.

NEW YORK SIDEWALKS

On we go, with the fast beat of traffic.
Gutted carcasses, with signs, on the side.
A balloon, celebrating an event:
It is too high for little hands to grab,
and low enough not to get sucked
into air conditioners.
The many merging, and I
Weave my heels with colored
Elastic bands, manufactured, and sent
To me as a child, in a box,
originally to make rainbowed woven potholders for
my mother,
I weave them through the crowds;
And we trip and stumble and regain our
Anonymous posture, with our gaze
Straight ahead, as we do not notice
Anyone standing, walking, sprinting, sitting,
leaning next to us.
The doctor's office stare at nothingness,
at pictures, billboards, displays;
and we display nothing.
We march our way to the curbs
And look out for potholes.

SHEEPLE

Rebel sheep, Unite!
Flock in your fleece
And give in to the
Conformist show.

Do not break the mold;
Do not go outside the lines.
Be pleased with your 9-5 job,
3 kids, happy spouse, stable future.

In the blindingly white wool
On your back,
be the populous in your country.
Hum the same tune,
go to bed at 9:30;
and continue to keep this world
safe
for the black sheep.

FALCON

What falcon did you send to block my path:
The bird of prey which stood protectively over
its kill; the needle talons piercing
the gray dove feathers.

CARNIVAL OF THE MOON

I breathe,
I work, now
on the game

I put the flowers into my mouth
And I chew and taste and eat.

Stuck in a festival
Of pink, green, red.
I see their cabbage-limp reply
In the carnival of the moon.

ILLEGAL DUMPING

„He left me again."
„How could he do this to me?"
or
„Was it something I did?"
She sleeps through lightning.
Her eyelids do not flicker, even
When thunder hits its crescendo.
The idyllic dreams that frolic
Through her slumbering mind
And dance on her naive eyes
Do not shield her from the rain;
Only the noise and the fury.
It was painful to listen
To my sister's pain.
To hear how he conquered her
Heart; how he promised better times,
happier days, fruitful harvests
when they sowed time together.
She, begrudgingly, discovered that he
Was just another politician.
Sure, her heart swelled with patriotism
For a while, during his term;
But was at a loss during the next
Elections. She thought, while gazing at
Reflections of past operatives,
if a female candidate would be
any better...or if a politician is
only that: sexless.
But, even more painful to hear was
His side: like clockwork,
at 6, at 11, and some in between,
just in case 6 or 11 wasn't enough.

Man versus man, again.
I see the same questions of denial,
blame-the same old „was-it-something-
I-said" routine. Checkmated cities,
overthrown governments and
sabotaged, classified, secret plots:
Plots of conquest,
plots of betrayal,
plots of introspection.
The blitzkrieg attack on the
News station was not my affair;
Nor my country's triangle, yet
They continued to banter
On and on –
Every night, light clockwork.
Every week, another liaison,
another break-up,
another travesty of the heart.
And every week, the story is
Dumped on my conscience,
like clockwork.
A war every few years,
like clockwork.
And, although I have tuned
Their tumultuous fury out,
their acid tears scathe my
slumbering skin, until only
their worming lies and „misleadings" will,
in my idyllic dream,
appear.

BUBBLES

We had coffee together.
I got my own black coffee from a pot,
and when I pushed, bubbles
were on the brew.

I sat with my coffee
At the table
Where he had his coffee.

He had some romantically sounding
Broth floating in his paper cup,
which was poured for him.
So there were no bubbles.

He reached over to strike my froth:

I stopped him.
I can pop my own bubbles.

EDINBURGH CASTLE

I was late, one mistful morning.
I forgot my jacket, I remembered my keys;
the morning consumed me, and I hardly saw the day
looming above my haze.

No Scottish brew would thin the gloom,
but it would warm my bare soul.

I left a note on your window, although some
letters were blurred from the morning dew.

The frost was receding from the year, and the
snowdrop flowers outside your garden were in bloom. Their
weary heads weeping thawed rime in rainbow puddles on the
paved path to your door.

I kept walking, preparing myself for a lonely day. I
could feel warmth in the fog, and felt the sun penetrating the
ache of the mist.

I walked beyond the shadow of your Edinburg Castle,
and headed home.

ABOUT THE AUTHOR

Tamarah Rockwood is a poet and the Founder and CEO of Bainbridge Island Press, an independent poetry publishing house. Her work has appeared in Brattle Street Review, New Verse Review, The Galway Review, Paddler Press, One Art, and Ultramarine Literary Review, among many others. Her poem "Coyotes Laughing" was longlisted for the 2019 University of Canberra Vice Chancellor's International Poetry Prize. She is the author of the poetry collection *A, B*.

A graduate of Harvard University with a degree in Creative Writing and Literature, Tamarah is Chair of Ars Poetica WA, a community that brings poets and artists together, and previously led Poetry Corners, an annual celebration of poetry and poets on Bainbridge Island. She has served as Chairwoman of the Literary Committee at Seattle's Rainier Club and as President of the Alumnae/i Network of Harvard Women. Currently a PhD candidate at the University of Birmingham, UK, she lives on Bainbridge Island, Washington, with her husband and five children.

www.ingramcontent.com/pod-product-compliance
Lightning Source LLC
Chambersburg PA
CBHW051328120626
46547CB00015B/2453